THE O'REALLY FACTOR

Everything's That's Right From A-Z!

by

David Samson

funnyguy.c m

Illustrated by

Jack Medoff

Specialist Press International

New York

DEDICATION:

To all those right wing Republicans-
-and chicken wing Democrats!

The O'Really Factor
Published by
The Funny Guy Company
and

SPECIALIST PRESS INTERNATIONAL

BOOK DESIGN, COVER DESIGN BY MARTIN ARCHER
COVER TYPE DESIGN BY DENISE LABELLE
ILLUSTRATIONS BY JACK MEDOFF

ISBN: 978-156171-214-4
Library of Congress Cataloging
in-Publication Data
Samson, David
The O'Really Factor

For any
additional information, visit:
www. FunnyGuy.com
and
www.spibooks.com
or contact:
publicity@spibooks.com
dave@funnyguy.com

THE FUNNYGUY.COM LIBRARY:

Available from bookstores everywhere!

(see book descriptions and ordering info at back of book)

How To Get God To Return Your Calls

The Joy of Depression

Men Who Hate Themselves:

(And The Women Who Agree With Them)

Wake Up And Smell The Coffin

American Idle

How To Be Funny When You Owe Money

Do Reality Checks Ever Bounce?

Masturbation for Morons

Useless Knowledge[1]

The Official Millennium Survival Handbook[2]

Is He For Real?[3]

Is He Mr. Right?[3]

The Middle Age of Aquarius

Love Codes[3]

1001 Ways You Reveal Your Personality[3]

1001 More Ways You Reveal Your Personality[3]

Parents Who Stay Lovers[3]

Rob Parr's Post-Pregnancy Workout[4]

Tammy Faye: Telling It My Way[5]

SAY YOUR PURRS! - 99 Ways To Misuse A Cat

1. With Joe Edelman
2. With Peter Bergman (of The Fire Sign Theatre)
3. With Dr. Elayne Kahn 4. With Rob Parr
5. With Tammy Faye Bakker

Specialist Press International titles are available at deep discounts when ordered in bulk quantities for premiums, promotions, fund raising or educational use. We can also create custom editions with your organization's name on them to your specs.

For further info please contact:

Special Sales Dept.

Specialist Press International

99 Spring Street • New York, New York 10012

sales@spibooks.com • Tel: 212-431-5011 • Fax: 212-431-4686

A

ABC
Don't be surprised when they do a morning show with four gay guys called "The Rear View"

ABORTION

I'm in favor of abortion - but only for Democrats. I believe their mothers should have the right to terminate them until they're 45 years old.

45 YEAR OLD FETUS

ACLU

They're the kind of scum who would sue Santa Claus for being a pedophile.

AFGHANISTAN

Pakistan, Kurdistan, Uzbekistan, apparently this guy Stan got around!

ANN COULTER

Here's a switch. An anorexic who makes liberals want to vomit!

AL QAEDA

Getting rid of them is a good start. Now let's get rid of all the other Als -- Al Gore, Al Sharpton -- and most of all, Al Franken!

B

BILL CLINTON
He had so many sex scandals they're thinking of renaming his Presidency the Bush Administration

BARACK OBAMA

From winning so many primaries, you can see this guy has become really conceited. So conceited, that I think he should have emergency liposuction on his ego.

BARBARA STREISAND

This radical left-winger really knows how to turn heads - away in revulsion.

BROOKLYN

The place where I was born. As I recall, my neighborhood was so tough that all the restaurants served broken leg of lamb.

BAR CODES

Women should be forced to wear them on dates. This way, guys could carry scanners and instantly see how much they're REALLY going to cost..

BET

If there's BET (the Black Entertainment Network), why not WET (the White Entertainment Network)? Is someone prejudiced out there?

BUDDHISTS

Did you hear about the Buddhist with the living will. It says "Please Don't Reincarnate."

**ONE MILLION B.C.
(BEFORE CLINTON)**

BEVERLY HILLS

It's populated by celebrity schizos who call Bush's environmental record a bummer -- especially when out driving their Hummers!

BIGOTRY

Let's get this straight. I don't hate people because of their race, religion or ethnic backgrounds, no matter how inferior their genes, beliefs, or countries of origin may be.

BISEXUALS

How about a catchy little slogan for them? For instance, sometimes you feel like a nut, sometimes you don't.

BLOGGING

What America obviously needs is less blogging and more logging!

BLEEDING HEART LIBERAL

Wasn't that David Letterman -- before his bypass surgery?

BRITNEY SPEARS

Secretly, a religious conservative. Rearrange the letters of her name and you get "Presbyterians" -- yeah, really!

C

CALIFORNIA
If the people living out there had any more depth, they'd be two dimensional.

CAR EMISSIONS

Thanks to higher standards, it now takes suicidal people three times longer to kill themselves. That must be tough -- especially for Dr. Kervokian!

ZERO EMISSIONS VEHICLE

CHINA

That country is getting more capitalistic all the time. Now I hear you can visit The Great Mall of China.

CLONING

I'm against cloning any human being, particularly Katie Couric.

KATIE COURIC - CLONED

CLUB MED

Just a bunch of over-rated tropical day care centers situated on third world beaches. In just a few more years, as the baby boomers hit retirement age, they should rename it Club Medicare.

CRACK DEALERS

In my neighborhood, they're all proctologists.

CAPITAL PUNISHMENT

I don't believe in it. Especially when you've accumulated over $10 million is capital and are being taxed at the highest rates. Now that's capital punishment!

CALLER ID

What we really need is Caller IQ. Let's you know if any morons are on the line.

CONDOMS

I have a great idea. How about Day-Glo condoms. It would give a whole new meaning to the phrase "You light up my life."

CONSERVATIVE WEDDINGS

I went to a conservative wedding last week. It was so conservative, they had an ice sculpture of Pat Buchanan

CNN

Oh, you mean the Communist News Network!

D

DEMOCRATS
Maybe they should go into the cellular business and offer the Flip-Flop phone!.

DALI LAMA

The spiritual leader of Tibet. But how did he land such a cushy job? My guess is that on his resume he lied about his Previous Life Experience.

DEMAGOGUE

A TV personality who gains power and popularity by arousing the emotions, passions and prejudices of people through totally distorting the truth. Is there something wrong with that?

DICK CHENEY

Next time he goes quail hunting, he should go after Dan Quayle. That would raise his popularity 75 points!

DIVERSITY

I have nothing against white women and Caucasian males freely associating with each other in an atmosphere of mutual respect and tolerance.

WHITE WOMAN AND CAUCASIAN MALE

DR. KEVORKIAN

Finally one of his patients is suing him for malpractice. Seems the guy lived.

DRUGS

My entire life has been drug-free. Of course, my uncle is a pharmacist.

DOMESTIC SPYING

You got to do it -- otherwise those maids and butlers are going to steal you blind!

DEATH PENALTY

How about The Execution Channel? Hangings, injections, electrocutions, all shown 24/7. You could have a panel of commentators called the Capital Punishment Gang. Even quiz shows where winners would get a stay of execution -- for 15 minutes!

E

ENGLAND

Socialism in action. The only country where people sneak into hospitals just for the food.

ENRON

Weren't they run into the ground by a UFO -- Unidentified Financial Officer?

ESP

At this stage of the game, it just stands for Eating, Sleeping, and Pooping.

ELLEN DEGENERIS

Excuse me. Shouldn't that be Ellen DeGenerate?

EMINENT DOMAIN

How about seizing the Supreme Court and turning it condo? Would serve them right - the pinheads!

E PLURIBUS UNUM

Our country's motto in Latin? Bad idea. Sounds like we're already part of Latin America.

EVANGELICAL CHRISTIANS

We're the base of The Republican Party. But thanks to the Democrats, we've become debased!

E-BAY

How do you sell a French rifle on E-bay?

Say it's never been fired and only dropped once!

ENVIRONMENTALISTS

Before the Heavens and Earth were created, they probably would have demanded that God file an environmental impact statement.

EVOLUTION

Our ancestors are monkeys? That's a crock that flies in the face of Divine Creation and all that is holy on earth. Although it would explain Democrats.

EQUAL RIGHTS AMENDMENT

It would affirm both women and men equally hold all of the rights guaranteed by the U. S. Constitution - unless they're smokers. Then they're screwed!

ERA NON-SUPPORTER

THE ENVIRONMENT? WHAT A CROC!

F

FAITH
Conservatives believe that we are all god's children. Oh yes, liberals believe that we are all god's children too -- from a previous marriage!

FEMINISTS

There's research saying they have a harder time conceiving than other women. Well, that makes sense. I guess their eggs are too hard boiled.

FAULTY INTELLIGENCE

One needn't look any further for examples than The New York Times.

FLAG BURNING

I support anyone who wants to burn the American flag. But first, they have to wrap themselves up in it.

FLAT TAX

Obviously, something Halle Barry will never have to worry about.

FAMILY VALUES

Net worth should be over $30 mil. Otherwise, they're NO family I value.

FRANCE

They call their jet fighter the Mirage – probably because it doesn't really exist.

HIT THE ROAD, JACQUES!

G

GENEVA CONVENTION
The hell with that. As a conservative, I'm not going to any convention unless it's held in Dallas!

GLOBAL WARMING

Eco-Fascists say the ice is melting. What a crock. The ice bucket in my limo is doing just fine!

GENOME PROJECT

Godless scientists who won't stop until they create a race of humans with designer genes!

GENETIC RESEARCHER
(WORKING A BUG OUT)

AL GORE

One thing about Al, he's BORED Certified!

GAY CHURCHES

You can always tell you've entered one, because only half the congregation is kneeling.

GERALDO RIVERA

I have nothing against that ultra-liberal political crusader who uses his media celebrity to undermine everything that's decent and wholesome about America. Nothing at all.

GAY MARRIAGE

What about gay divorce? No one ever talks about that. When two guys get divorced, will one of them collect Palimony. When about lesbians, will they call it *Galimony* ?

GAYS IN THE MILITARY

I think it's a great idea -- especially when you want to attack from the rear!

GREENHOUSE GASES

We could eliminate 90% of deadly emissions simply by declaring Mexican food illegal, if you catch my drift here.

GUANTANAMO

American naval base in Cuba where suspected terrorists are subjected to cruel and unusual punishments, such as water boarding or watching speeches by Michael Dukakis.

GUN RACKS

You can tell that crazy liberals run California. They absolutely don't allow gun racks in trucks, just wine racks.

G SPOT

Believe me, I know where that G spot is. You know you've hit it when a woman screams out, "GEE, you're not wearing those underwear again!" "GEE, put the toilet seat down!" "GEE, get off of me already!" "GEE, you're married?"

GURU

The only guru I'd ever listen to would have his loincloth decked out in corporate logos. That's what I call a real Prophet Motive!

PROPHET MOTIVE

H

HILLARY
CLINTON
I absolutely have no objection
to a woman becoming and
serving as President -
- of the PTA!

HELL

According to scripture, the place of eternal damnation reserved for self-righteous non-smokers!

NON-SMOKER'S HELL

HILLARY CLINTON (CIRCA 1967)

HEALTH INSURANCE

Never mind that. How about wealth insurance? This way if I drop a couple of mil in the stock market, Allstate has to pay through the nose!

HILLARY CLINTON

She's the type of woman you could bring home to your mother. If your mother was a lesbian.

HOMELESS PEOPLE

I applaud liberals who want to throw parties for homeless people...but I just have one question. Where do they mail all the invitations?

HOMOPHOBIA

Let me say that's completely ridiculous. I have absolutely no fear of returning home.

HETEROSEXUALS

The union between them is the most blessed and joyful on earth, providing they have no in-laws, car payments, or cold sores.

HOWARD DEAN

Democrats have as their party's symbol the donkey. Guess who's the ass?

HIROSHIMA

What's the difference between North Korea and Hiroshima? Nothing...yet.

HURRICANE KATRINA

From what I can see, it did 27 billion dollars worth of improvements!

HITLER

Would he have put people with Attention Deficit Disorder into Lack of Concentration Camps? Just a thought.

I

IOWA
Ever wonder why they call it the Iowa Caucus - - because the people are all Caucasians!

IRS

Liberals now want deductions for NOT having children. They claim kids use up vital resources like air, water, and Hershey's bars. So the more you don't have, the bigger your deduction. What pinheads!

INFOMERCIALS

On TV they want you to dial these 800 numbers, but lots of them are actually using convicts in prison as operators. I wonder if they're taking calls on their cell phones?

IMAGINARY PLAYMATES

I admit it. I had one growing up. Of course, that was an imaginary Playmate of the Month!

IRAQI WAR

You know the reason Bush sent women with PMS to fight in the desert -- because they're mad as hell AND they retain water!

IRAN

A country full of Sunnis with leaders full of Shi'ite!

INDIA

When I call up my cable or credit card company I want to speak to Indiana -- not India! Speaking to an American. Has that become a foreign concept?

THE INQUISITION

A great period in history. A time when liberals really got into hot water!

DISPOSING OF A LIBERAL (CIRCA 1571 AD)

ILLEGAL IMMIGRATION

We don't need to build a wall. Let's buy the one the Chinese already have and put IT on the border.

ILLEGAL ALIENS IN THE WORKPLACE

J

JOHN KERRY
He has a plan for paying off the national debt. He's putting it on his wife's Gold card.

JENNIFER FLOWERS

That's one promiscuous broad. From what my sources tell me, Bill Clinton used to reach her by dialing 1-800-FLOWERS.

JERRY GARCIA

Attention all you drugged-out freaks. Jerry is now listed in "The Tibetan Book of the Grateful Dead."

JESSE JACKSON

Jesse was heard saying that he wanted to cut Barack Obama's nuts off - and he wasn't talking about pistachios, my friends!

J. EDGAR HOOVER

Let's get the facts straight. Just because you're a perverted cross-dresser doesn't mean you can't be patriotic!

J. EDGAR HOOVER

JEWS FOR JESUS

Not a bad idea. They could go to confession every time they buy retail and say 100 "Hail Macy's"

JIMMY CARTER

Weak-kneed appeaser of the Mullahs in Iran and supreme saboteur of our nation's war on terrorism. And those are just his good points!

JERRY FALWELL

Founder of the Moral Majority, he claimed that God spoke to him every night. Unfortunately, God called collect!

JOE LIEBERMAN

Senator from Connecticut and close personal friend of mine. A staunch supporter of Israel, a strong national defense, and upholder of traditional American values, such as making sure drug and insurance companies can charge whatever the hell they want. That's my boy!

JOHN EDWARDS

He claims there are two America's - one rich, one poor. But like all bleeding heart liberals, Edwards is a lying adulterer with the moral values of a wildebeest. A sinner who reportedly paid his mistress $100,000 for sex. Yeah, that certainly lifted her out of poverty!

JOHN KERRY

No one can possibly question the fact that he volunteered to go off and fight in Vietnam - on the side of the North!

JOB SECURITY

Another ultra-liberal concept. In my opinion, you get more out of sluggish workers with job insecurity.

JOB INSECURITY

JAPANESE

They launched a sneak attack on Pearl Harbor in violation of every treaty and agreement they ever signed. Okay, I forgive them that. Through World War II they killed or tortured hundreds of thousands of brave Americans under the most monstrous conditions imaginable. Okay, I forgive them that. Then they deliberately wrecked our economy and destroyed millions of high-paying American jobs with their Toyotas and Hondas and Nissans. Okay, I forgive them that. ...But for sushi? Never!!!

JOHN MCCAIN

Presidential hopeful and hot-headed maverick who could order Armageddon on a moment's notice. At last - the candidate we've been praying for!

K

KENTUCKY FRIED CHICKEN
How about a special deal for conservatives? A bucket of chicken - - but only right wings!

KIM JONG IL

The North Korea Dictator is developing long range nuclear missiles capable of wiping out San Francisco. Finally, some good news!

KU KLUX KLAN

I hear they just adopted a highway. Problem is they're only picking up white trash.

K STREET

Where big lobbying firms in Washington DC spend millions of dollars buying corrupt politicians. My question -- why can't they just lease them instead?

LARRY KING

He's so old women ask him, "Is that a catheter in your pocket or are you just happy to see me?"

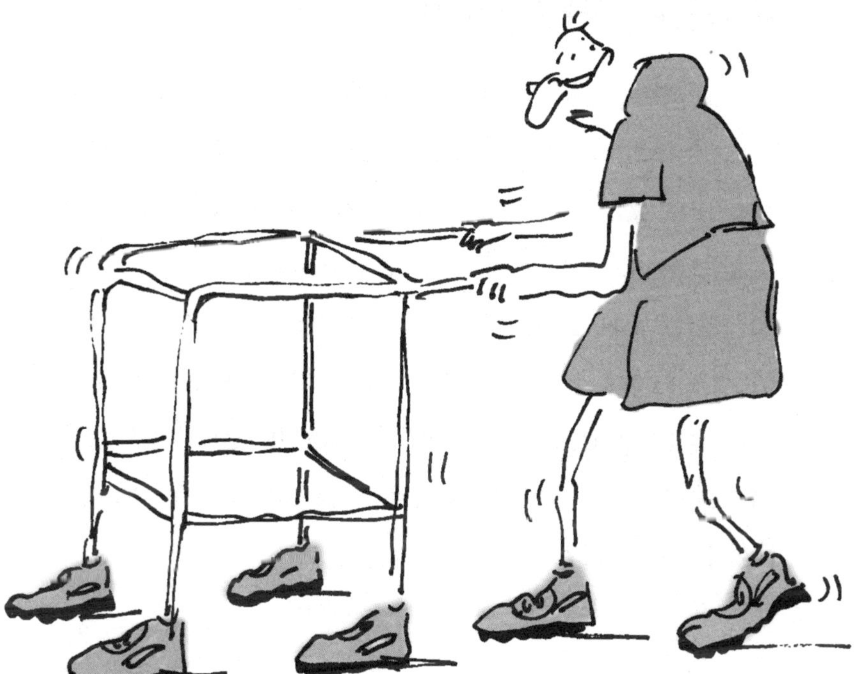

LARRY KING LIVE (WELL, ALMOST)

KGB

As former Secret Police they make perfect cab drivers. Just give them your name -- they already know where you live!

KABBALAH

A secret Jewish sect whose mystical teachings are followed by Madonna, Demi Moore and plenty of other Hollywood pinheads. To deflect envious stares and ill will, they must wear special bracelets made from red string around their wrists. The string costs them 26 bucks. 26 BUCKS! What's next for these nitwits? A lucky Rabbi's foot?

K-MART

Millions of Americans shop at K-Mart. But we need millions more to shop there! Let's look at the facts. K-mart produces everything they sell in China. They pump billions into the Chinese economy. Money the Chinese then lend back to us at exorbitant rates so that we can buy Arab oil at exorbitant prices to fill up our God-given trucks and SUVs. Get where I'm going here? Shop at K-Mart immediately! It's a matter of national security. Because in my opinion, there's still too many of those mom and pop shops still around destroying the American economy - how unpatriotic!

L

LAX
When terrorists finally blow it up,
what are they going to call it -
- EX-LAX?

LETTING GO

What corporations should do with ungrateful employees – from about 40 stories up!

I'M AFRAID WE'RE GOING TO HAVE TO LET YOU GO, PERKINS!

LEGALIZE

I have no problem granting citizenship to the 12 million illegal immigrants living in this country – right after we deport 12 million Democrats!

LOS ANGELES

NASA is recruiting people from Los Angeles to be the first astronauts to Neptune. No wonder. I bet they'll feel right at home in a toxic methane/ammonia atmosphere!

LSD

For Baby Boomers, it now means Low Sodium Diet.

LIBERALS

I love to have them for lunch - a piece at a time!

FORK ALL LIBERALS!

M

MONICA LEWINSKY
She had a great opportunity as a White House intern -
- then she blew it!

MAD COW DISEASE

The way these idiots on Wall Street operate, I'm more worried about Mad Dow Disease!

MAFIA

From what my contacts inside the Justice Department tell me, the Italian Mafia no longer a problem. The problem is the Jewish-Mafia. Otherwise know as "The Kosher Nostra." They put a price on your head and then they mark it down!

MAINSTREAM MEDIA

CBS, NBC, ABC, all the major networks are controlled by crazed liberal programmers conducting secret meetings every Tuesday night with the sole aim of destroying the morals of America and depleting our very will to survive. Not that I'm paranoid.

MARIJUANA

Know what I call any left winger who wants to legalize marijuana? Harry Potted!

HARRY POTTED

MALIBU

The bad news is that one woman residing there was recently buried under a mudslide and died; the good news is that the corpse had the best-looking skin you've ever seen!

MICHAEL JACKSON

George Bush's educational program is "Leave No Child Behind." I'm afraid Michael's is "Leave no child's behind."

MICHAEL MOORE

A far left ideologue committed to spreading the most vicious lies about the Bush administration. He also recently went down on Fidel Castro.

MIDDLE CLASS

Millions of whiners and moaners who demand tax cuts and college tuition. Let me tell you something. Back in the Feudal Ages they didn't even HAVE a middle class and those societies worked just fine. See where I'm going here...

MID EAST

We should immediately send a million troops to destroy every last radical in the Mid East -- particularly those in Vermont and Massachusetts!

MITT ROMNEY

Let me tell you one thing. If that Mormon ever gets elected, he'll be the first President with SEVEN first ladies!

M

N

NORTH KOREA
Wouldn't surprise me if the French have already surrendered to them.

RALPH NADER

Anti-Corporate fanatic dedicated to bringing down the entire capitalist system. He ran for President in 2000 and drained off enough votes in Florida from Al Gore to throw the election to George Bush. Way to go, Ralphie boy!

NANCY PELOSI

The first woman to be speaker of the House. What are you kidding me? EVERY woman is speaker of the house!

NATIVE AMERICANS

We slaughtered them by the millions and stole their land. Now they're trying to steal their land back using their Indian casinos. Let's face it. Though they didn't invent the wheel, they sure know how to use the roulette wheel!

NAZIS

I may be getting paranoid, but my sources tell me there's this top secret group of Non-verbal Nazis running around. They can't be wiretapped by the FBI because they don't ever talk. But I know how to spot them. Because they're the ones reading "Mime Kampf."

NEGATIVE ADS

Political advertising that intentionally smears opponents through false statements, such as saying all Democrats are drug dealing child molesters. Whoops, bad example.

NEIGHBORHOODS

Thanks to liberal judges and parole boards, all your neighbors probably are hoods!

RICHARD NIXON

Just what we need -- another Dick in the White House!

NEO-CONSERVATIVES

An extreme group of right wingers that wants to attack any country posing even the slightest threat to America. Canada, for example.

NOSTRADAMUS

Amazing psychic who predicted the notorious careers of Napoleon, Hitler, Stalin and Dennis Kucinich.

NEWT GINGRICH

The former House Speaker who created a mandate for Republicans, though not necessarily what Senator Larry Craig considers a man date.

NSA

A top secret government agency accused of tapping phones without a warrant and violating the most fundamental aspects of our constitutional democracy. What's the problem here?

NUCLEAR WASTE

Any bombs we DON'T drop on Iran!

NUDE BEACHES

Years ago I went to one. It was disgusting. Everywhere I looked, women were always DRESSING me with their eyes!

O

OSAMA BIN LADEN
I hear he's forming a new country western band - - The Islamic GEEEEE-Had!!

OIL SPILLS

It sickens me to see those dead birds covered in black gook.

Such a waste of good crude!

OIL COMPANIES

A ruthless cartel of mega-corporations responsible for gouging hard-working Americans at the pump. Way to go!

OPEC

The petroleum producing nations of the Middle East who are notorious for paying off terrorists and torturing their own people. I can't stand that – the paying off terrorists part.

ORGAN TRANSPLANTS

Why stop with organs? Let's take those thousands of child molesters and rapists relaxing in prison and recycle ALL their parts. Maybe even start a chain of body shops!

KEITH OLBERMAN

Fanatical host of "Countdown" on MSNBC, a raving liberal who defames me every night with the most slanderous and vicious lies ever told on the air. But nonetheless I admire Keith. And his live-in lover, Chris Matthews.

OUTSOURCING

A great way to teach all those pesky labor leaders who's the boss!

OPRAH WINFREY

As a person of European descent, I have always supported other people of pure European descent for the Presidency of the United States. But since Obama has a white mother, I've decided to offer him HALF my support. So you see Oprah, I've finally met you 50% of the way!

P

PASSOVER

For over 400 years the Jews were in bondage in Egypt until Moses set them free. There was only one small problem. Some of those Jews were really into bondage.

PANTYHOSE

What's the similarity between Iran and pantyhose? They both irritate Bush.

SARAH PALIN

Staunch defender of Alaskan sovereignty against Eskimo uprisings, moose invasions, Polar Bear incursions and penguin infestation. I saw the video of her competing in the Miss Alaska beauty pageant. Now that's Northern

Exposure! What I like is she supports off-shore drilling - even for dentists. And with McCain now at her side, she's gone from the bridge to nowhere to the BRIDGEWORK to nowhere!

PAST LIFE THERAPY

Come on! What do these wackos expect you to do? Talk about your parents -- your parents in the Babylonian Era?

PAT ROBERTSON

My good friend Pat has achieved national and international recognition as a religious broadcaster, philanthropist, educator, businessman and author. For some reason, he has yet to pick up the check.

PATRIOT ACT

That's what I call Howard Dean, Jane Fonda and Michael Moore when they pretend to love America!

PEDOPHILE PRIESTS

Why can't these guys simply go into therapy and get themselves pedicured!

PRESCRIPTION DRUG PLAN

Making the government shell out billions for all those old geezer's medications -- that idea should have been buried immediately -- together with the recipients!

POLITICS

From "poli" in Latin meaning "many" and "tics" meaning "bloodsucking vermin".

PLO

A bunch of crazed suicide bombers who want to force Jews to return to their ancestral home: Miami Beach.

PRO-LIFE

I am definitely Pro-Life, Pro-War, Pro-Hockey and Pro-Wrestling. Guess that makes me a Total Pro!

Q

QUAGMIRE
A dangerous situation from which it is difficult to extract oneself, such as the war in Iraq or cocktails with James Carville.

QUEERS

They obviously run the liberal media. Otherwise, we'd have shows in prime time like "Straight Eye for the Queer Guy".

STRAIGHT EYE FOR THE QUEER GUY

QUOTAS

No employer should show the slightest preference to any racial, ethnic or religious group – except for Pure White Protestants. Then it's okay.

QUAKERS

Folks who've chosen to lead pastoral lives of mutual support and non-violence sequestered away from the corruption of modern existence make me mad, for some reason.

QUID PRO QUO

The notion of giving something in exchange for something else. For example, Democrats selling out their country for a few Madonna tickets.

R

ROSIE O'DONNELL
She should put a webcam in her bedroom and people will pay her millions -
- NOT to turn it on!

RONALD REAGAN

After Reagan left office, he got an office building and an airport named after him. What's Clinton going to get? A daycare center and fertility clinic?

REPUBLICANS

They won the last election by shrewdly appealing to the bisexual vote -- why else would they nominate Bush and Dick?

RUSH LIMBAUGH

A man after my own heart. And with his cholesterol, he's probably after my liver and kidneys as well!

RECYCLING

I recycle all my newspapers. I leave them in the bathroom stall when I'm done.

RAP MUSIC

No wonder they call it Rap Music. These pinheads all have rap sheets a mile long.

RELATIONSHIPS

Women may be from Venus, but let's remember folks, Men Still Have The Penis!

RELIGIOUS CONSERVATIVES

God-fearing folk who know that Satan will never be allowed in the Republican party – and neither will Barney Frank!

REAGAN DEMOCRATS

Staunch Americans who still mourn the loss of the former President, plus certain key teeth.

S

SEX
Liberals are so politically correct. You know how they make love - - both people on top!

SADDAM HUSSEIN

An unscrupulous manic who employed the most unspeakable methods to seize political power and remain there. I'm sorry, I was talking about Karl Rove.

SAN FRANCISCO

Seems they found this hive of killer bees up there -- One drone and fifty million queens!

SEPARATION OF CHURCH AND STATE

Liberals constantly remind us that God is neither a Republican nor a conservative. Oh yeah, since when?

SAUDI ARABIA

A country that's 90% desert is a great place to ship liberals, since they love sticking their heads in the sand anyway!

ANOTHER LIBERAL STICKING HIS NECK OUT!

SEANCES

In Los Angeles, people go to them just to get in touch with the living!

SEXUAL HARASSMENT

I don't care what all those muck-raking commentators and newspapers are saying. I NEVER touched her ass!

STEM CELL RESEARCH

Let's stem it now! These cell phones are complicated enough!

SCHOOL PRAYER

Conservatives want to put prayer into the schools. Well, I don't know about you, but the way the schools are now, with all the guns and violence, I think it would be a better idea to say your prayers before you get to school. "Please, I just want to live. Don't shoot me..." Right?

SOCIALIZED MEDICINE

A far left disaster that would drive millions of Americans across the Mexican border for medical care, mark my word!

SWEET 'N' LOW

Thanks to which, I now have Low Blood Saccharin.

SECRET WIRETAPPING

Beyond a doubt, the government does not have the right to secretly wiretap American citizens. Except for those watching my competition, of course

SOCIAL SECURITY

The hell with that commie concept! I believe in Social Insecurity! Why should all those freeloading geezers get all the gravy? Big bucks that could be better spent building roads and bridges and schools and factories all across the entire nation - of Iraq!

T

THE TALIBAN
These inhuman barbarians force women to cover their bodies from head to toe. Send them Barbra Streisand immediately!

TED KENNEDY

Didn't he once have a favorite song - Bridge Over Troubled Waters?

THE HOMELESS

You know what I'd give them? A subscription to "Better Homes & Cartons"

KISS MY ASSETS!

TEHRAN

What's the weather forecast for Tehran? Administration insiders tell me that it's going to be 9000 degrees and overcast.

THERAPY

Here I want to see the kind of same advances the auto-insurance industry has made -- No-Fault Therapy. This way, you only go in for one session and your shrink tells you that neither you nor your parents or your teachers, lovers, husbands, wives were to blame and you walk out cured for seventy-five bucks flat. Great concept, huh?

THE GAZA STRIP

Isn't that a PLO Nudist Club or something?

TORTURE

The act of locking up suspected terrorists and subjecting them repeatedly to Barry Manilow.

THE TEN COMMANDMENTS

They should be displayed in every court in the nation, including food courts and tennis courts!

TERRORIST WATCH LIST

If the French had their way, they'd give Saddam a Rolex and Osama a Timex.

TSUNAMIS

Let's say a tidal wave wipes out Tokyo. So what? As they say in Japan, "Shitake Happens!"

THE CHOSEN PEOPLE

Great advertising line. Competitive. Punchy. To the point. Clearly demonstrates market superiority. Everything you always wanted in a religion -- and less. Less Gods than anyone else. In fact, just One! That's one stop praying my friends. So stop messing around with hundreds of deities with hearts of stone and get with the program. Boy, what a terrific concept! Now what about those Eskimos? God's Frozen People? Just a thought.

TRICKLE-DOWN ECONOMICS

Only seems to work if you have bladder problems.

U

UNITED NATIONS
Every nation in the world belongs to it except the Vatican. Jesus, they're smart!

UNBORN

As far as I'm concerned, the unborn have rights – like the right to bear arms. I say give that fetus a fighting chance!

UNIVERSAL HEALTHCARE

If Universal wants to give their employees medical insurance, that's fine with me. Same goes for Paramount and Disney.

UN-AMERICAN

Any activity seeking to plot the overthrow of the United States government and its legally elected representatives in Washington, unless Democrats are in power.

UNION OF THE SOVIET SOCIALIST REPUBLICS

An obsolete regime ruled by pathetic old men – much like our unions.

UNEMPLOYMENT

Here's my solution. Start sneaking American farm workers into Mexico!

UCLA

Rearrange the letters and you get ACLU. Need I say anymore?

US OPEN

That's the problem. The US is TOO open. Any day now, terrorists could lob major volleys -- and I don't mean tennis balls!

V

VICTORY
Liberals have four synonyms for it:
Run, Hide,
Surrender,
or Collaborate.

VIETNAM

The difference between the Vietnam War and the Iraq War was that George W. Bush had a plan for getting out of the Vietnam War.

VALIUM

A tranquilizer proven highly effective in alleviating anxiety caused by Democratic gains and the Dixie Chicks.

V-CHIP

A piece of technology built into TV sets to protect young children from being exposed to violence. I don't get it. Then how will they ever learn?

VIAGRA

It's the patriotic drug. Makes you stand up for America. I only have one question. Does it come with an extended warranty?

THE VIAGRA PATRIOTS PARTY

VICTORIA'S SECRET

A filthy, perverted place for promiscuous women who have no sense of common morality or decency. They should rename it "Victoria's Secretions." By the way, I wouldn't be surprised if gays didn't soon come out with a store called "Victorio's Secret!"

VIRGINS

I am firmly and absolutely against pre-marital sex.

Post-marital sex is no picnic either!

VIRGIN ISLANDS

When I was growing up, these were Long Island and Staten Island, respectively.

W

WASHINGTON

With all the sexual perverts in Congress, they should rename it Washington AC/DC.

WOMEN'S RIGHTS

Pretty good. And some of them also have mean lefts.

WHITE TRASH

It should definitely be recycled, starting with Jessica Simpson.

WOODSTOCK

I think it's important to remember the lasting value of Woodstock. Which is why I want everyone to go out and buy shares in a lumber company.

WEAPONS OF MASS DESTRUCTION

A-Bombs set to go off in your All-Bran – sure, you laugh now!

X

X CHROMOSOME
Add a Y chromosome and you have a man. Add a K-Y chromosome and you have Elton John.

XENOPHOBIA

The completely irrational fear of foreign people, their customs or culture. On second thought, make that RATIONAL fear!

XYLOPHONE

It produces pleasing sounds when struck repeatedly with a mallet – much like a terrorist does.

X-FILES

A program dedicated to exposing the danger of hostile aliens taking over the U.S. Government. Sounds more like an amnesty program to me!

XANADU

An idyllically beautiful place devoid of the miseries that commonly beset humanity, such as Hillary Clinton and Harry Reid.

X-RATED WEB SITES

Those should all be turned into WEB sites!

Y

YOUNG REPUBLICANS

Starry-eyed idealists who believe that people everywhere are entitled to the American Dream, provided they first attended Cornell, Dartmouth, or Yale.

YOKO ONO

What do the Iraqi army and Yoko Ono have in common? They're both living off of dead beetles!

YUPPIES

Ruthless social climbers who would sell out their own mothers for a BMW or bottle of Dom Perignon. My kind of people!

YASSER ARAFAT

The most dangerous enemy the state of Israel has ever had (next to Mel Gibson).

Y2K

Intense paranoia spread by anti-corporate left wingers that all the computers around the world were going to crash, except for Bill Gates' laptop.

YELLOW CABS

Driven by unwashed cretins who refuse to pick up any minority group, bless their hearts. No wonder I have NO problem getting a taxi in New York City!

Z

ZZZZZZZ'S
A slang expression describing the state of deep sleep often induced by C-SPAN.

ZOMBIE

A soulless dead body brought back to life again. Sounds like Dr. Phil to me..

ZERO TOLERANCE

I believe in showing no leniency towards anyone engaged in behavior dangerous to society, such as drunk driving or demonstrating peacefully.

ZINFANDEL

A kind of red wine grown primarily in California. No wonder it's so fruity!

ZAPPING

How the government plans to kill bacteria in imported fruits and vegetables using high levels of radiation. Just what we need. Broccoli that glows in the dark!

ZUCCHINI

I once had a dream in which a zucchini was writing fan mail to John Kerry, another vegetable.

ZERO GRAVITY

In my opinion, the weight of all liberal arguments taken collectively.

ZONKED

Someone who is unconscious, stupefied or sleeping as a result of overexposure to drugs, alcohol or Wolf Blitzer.

ZODIAC

My personal astrologer predicts that Ameri ca - thanks to left wingers like Senator Joe Biden - will remain the most powerful nation on the planet, right after China, Russia, Lebanon and Lichtenstein.

ZENITH

Reaching the most incredible climax, though from my experience, not after an evening with Condoleezza Rice.

ZINGER

A sharp and perfectly timed witticism. For instance, Hollywood liberals like Alec Baldwin, Harry Belafonte, Sandra Bernhard, Susan Sarandon, Martin Sheen and Oliver Stone are all in touch with reality, but it's a long distance call!

ZERO INTEREST

What Americans should show the Democratic Party!

POLITICAL INACTIVIST!

ZIP CODES

The richest zip codes in America are 06830, 10022, 07901, 30327, and 90272. By coincidence, John McCain and I own houses in all of them!

ZEPPELIN

A huge blimp filled with gas - not unlike Ed Asner!

ZEALOT

An extremist dedicated to a revolutionary cause, a raving fanatic who wants to destroy the core principles that we Americans hold dearest, as contained in the Constitution, the Declaration of Independence, as well as my talking points memos.

ZEUS

In Greek Mythology, the greatest god that ever existed, supreme ruler of the cosmos and spiritual father of every being on earth. Sounds like my job definition!

A is for author–
David Samson

WHO IS FUNNYGUY.COM?

David Samson is a nationally known speaker, media personality, and the author of twenty-one books. His books have been published by The Penguin Group, Random House, Simon & Schuster, St. Martin's Press, among other major New York houses.

They've been seen on *David Letterman, The Today Show, Rosie 'O' Donnell, Live with Regis and Kathy Lee, Geraldo Rivera, Politically Incorrect, ABC Prime Time Live, The Fox News Network, Comedy Central, Entertainment Tonight, Donahue,* and *Larry King Live*.

His work has been featured or he's been interviewed in *People, Penthouse, Cosmopolitan, The New York Daily News, The Chicago Tribune, The Christian Science Monitor, The Philadelphia Metro, Los Angeles Magazine, USA Today,* plus *The New York Times*. His books are also translated around the world.

David is a frequent guest on major radio shows including top ten national markets of *ABC, CBS, FOX, Clear Channel, Westwood One, Radio America,* and *Pacifica Broadcasting*.

A former creative executive at some of America's largest advertising agencies, David often consults with clients in the marketing and PR spheres. He is also a professional member of the National Speaker's Association, talking to audiences across the country on topics from advertising and publishing to dating and relationships.

David watches network and cable news nonstop. He obviously needs help!

DEAR READER:

If you liked (or disliked) this book, please review the following pages for descriptions and ordering information on the other fine works in this series!

Funnyguy.com books are available in select bookstores around the world. If you can't get them at your favorite local bookshop, please use the order form that is provided. On U.S. orders that you mail in or fax, we will pay the shipping! On orders outside of the U.S., please add shipping of: $5.95 for the first book and $1.00 for each added book.

Thank You!

The Publisher

Get The Entire Funnyguy.com Library!

and at

spibooks.com

☐ **AMERICAN IDLE**
THE ANTI-MOTIVATION HANDBOOK

by David Samson

Make "Positive Thinking" a thing of the past! David Samson is "The Master of Poor Performance." Martha Stewart and Donald Trump haven't consulted with him – but you should! So overcome feelings of optimism! Achieve the stagnation you deserve! And remember those two little words that will forever set you free: WHY BOTHER? **$11.95**

☐ HOW TO Be Funny When You Owe Money

by David Samson

Scared to answer the phone? Don't worry! Because now when they ask for money, all you do is act funny. Just play the special sound effects CD when they call. You'll have a ball! Learn The CIA Paranoia Ploy; The Farting Fiasco; The Multiple Personality Maneuver; and many more! With David Samson's guidance you'll never hang up on another creditor. Cause you'll be giving them all the Hang-Ups! DVD and Free CD: $14.95 - Book and Free CD: **$11.95**

☐ MASTURBATION FOR MORONS
A DO-IT-YOURSELF HANDBOOK
by David Samson

The very first book for Mono-Sexuals! Find out why two people are one person too many. How to be your own best lover. The issue of Mono-Sexual marriage. Avoiding stains on your reputation. What to do when things get out of hand. Stiffening your resolve in the face of adversity. Yes, this is one handbook you won't be able to put down! **$11.95**

☐ THE JOY OF DEPRESSION

by David Samson

Depression is much more than a state-of-mind. It's a total way of living! And the perfect way to cope with all the stress of modern life. Learn the secrets of financial insecurity. Project negative charisma. Overcome the effects of a healthy childhood! Plus always remember: The best years of your life are still behind you! **$11.95**

☐ **MEN WHO HATE THEMSELVES**
—AND THE WOMEN WHO AGREE WITH THEM
by David Samson

Here's the truth about Living, Loving, and Loathing! Why men suffer from PMS (Pre-Marital Syndrome). What "The Male Lie-Bido" has to say. Plus advice from Dr. Baby Ruth; Buy-Sexuality in Women; Aero-Phobics for Men; Impersonal Ads; and much more! **$11.95**

☐ WAKE UP AND SMELL THE COFFIN

by David Samson

Are you reading Chicken Soup for the Departed Soul? Is Weed Killer now more important than Killer Weed? Has LSD come to mean Low Sodium Diet? Have you joined a 12 Step Program just to get up twelve steps? Are the Grateful Dead friends of yours who've visited Dr. Kevorkian? Then congratulations! This is the right book for you! **$11.95**

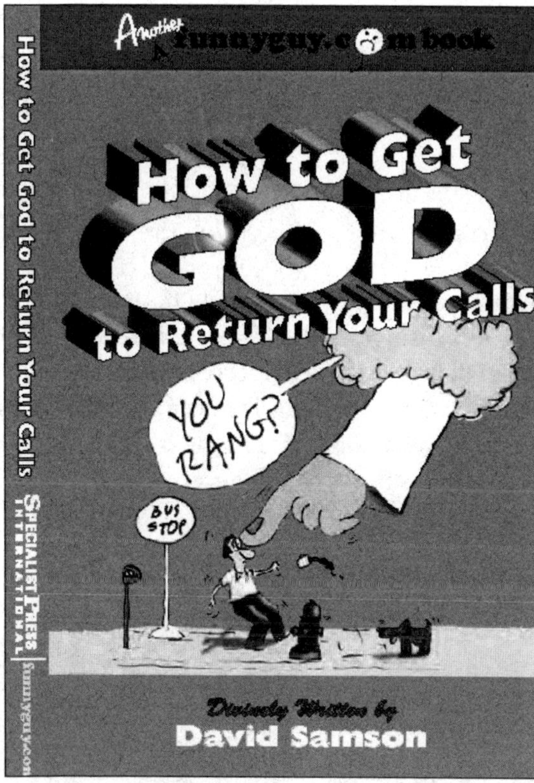

☐ **HOW TO GET GOD TO RETURN YOUR CALLS**

by David Samson

Feeling disconnected from God? Suspect your calls never even go through? Paranoid about being snubbed at the Heavenly Level? Well, worry no longer! Learn how to access God's private line. Cut through Cosmic Clutter and top His "Must Get Back To Immediately" list. Hundreds of proven techniques to get the answers you deserve! **$11.95**

☐ **IS HE FOR REAL?**
Knowing Sooner What A Man Will Be Like Later

by David Samson and Dr. Elayne Kahn
Separate the cream from the creeps! Because here, using the same methods as FBI profilers, men's secret signals about love and romance are finally exposed! This powerful and amusing book is spiced with intimate details. Know exactly what kind of lover he is – before going to bed. Now get the love you desire -- the love you deserve! **$11.95**

☐ **IS HE MR. RIGHT?**
How To tell If You Should Love Him or Leave Him

by David Samson and Dr. Elayne Kahn
Separate the cream from the creeps! Because here, using the same methods as FBI profilers, men's secret signals about love and romance are finally exposed! This powerful and amusing book is spiced with intimate details. Know exactly what kind of lover he is – before going to bed. Now get the love you desire -- the love you deserve! **$11.95**

☐ DO REALITY CHECKS EVER BOUNCE?
Knowing Sooner What A Man Will Be Like Later

Illustrated by Martin Archer

Is your inner child adopted? Can white trash be recycled? Do cold fronts have warm behinds? Should liver transplants come with onions? Obviously, these can't be answered by any person -- any sane person! Plus each outrageous page is hilariously illustrated. You won't be able to stop laughing! **$9.95**

☐ THE OFFICIAL POST-MILLENNIUM SURVIVAL HANDBOOK
by David Samson and Peter Bergman

You're not out of the woods yet! Find out what you need to know all way up to the year 2999. Because the new Millennium will be an equal opportunity annihilator. Lawyers, arsonists, dentists will all find themselves in the same boat as you -- namely the Titanic! Written with Peter Bergman of the legendary Firesign Theater! Obviously, these can't be answered by any person -- any sane person! Plus each outrageous page is hilariously illustrated. You won't be able to stop laughing! **$9.95**